REBECCA CLARK

The Bride's Guide: How to Plan Your Wedding Day Timeline

Plan your dream wedding day with ease! Eliminate stress, gain peace of mind, and enhance your overall wedding day experience, even if you don't have a wedding planner.

This book was professionally typeset on Reedsy.
Find out more at reedsy.com

Contents

1

Introduction

Planning a wedding can be very overwhelming and stressful. What's supposed to be the happiest time of your life, can end up being a total nightmare.

This guide is crafted to support you in planning your dream wedding day with ease! By following this step-by-step approach, you can eliminate stress, gain peace of mind, and enhance your overall wedding day experience, even if you don't have a wedding planner or coordinator.

I'm Rebecca Clark! My husband and I have been filming weddings since 2015 and photographing weddings since 2019. I put this guide together using the best of my knowledge, experience, and expertise in working and planning weddings and elopements.

The most common question I see couples asking is, "How do I create my wedding day timeline?". You spend about 80% of your wedding day with your photographer and videographer so why not use a guide that was created by a wedding photographer and videographer?

This is not meant to replace your wedding planner or coordinator. We always recommend you hire one of those vendors. But if you'd like to get the ball rolling with planning or simply cannot afford to hire one, you'll find that this guide is a huge help!

I want to preface, this guide is exactly that, a guide. No two weddings are the same, and they shouldn't be. This means you don't *have* to do all the wedding traditions just because the rest of your friends or family did or just because it's listed as an option in this guide. This is YOUR day. Plan your day however you'd like it to be! It can be as laid back or as planned out as you want!

As you read through this guide, go in with the mindset that everything doesn't need to be exactly perfect. I promise you, you'll have a much happier wedding day experience if you just say, "It's not the end of the world", if something doesn't go according to plan.

Now, rest easy, take a breath, and be sure to jot down questions and create a to-do list as you read.

Okay! Let's jump right in!

2

Where To Start

To begin planning out your timeline, I recommend finding out what time the sun is going to set for your chosen wedding day and then work your way backwards from there. For example, if the sun is going to set at 7:30 pm, we suggest beginning your ceremony at least 3 hours before the sun sets, which would be 4:30 pm. Then you'd continue working backwards until you reach "getting ready" start time. You can skip to Chapter Two: "Ceremony Start Time" if you'd like, or you can continue reading in order starting with Chapter One.

3

Pre-Ceremony

"Pre-Ceremony" will include all the events and moments starting from the point you begin getting ready to the point where your ceremony begins.

Getting Ready

(Approximately 1-3 hours recommended)

The "Getting Ready" portion usually consists of all the events taking place *before* everyone is fully dressed. It can start as early as you want. It can start with you and your fiance having breakfast together to shake off the nerves or you and your mom/dad/parents/siblings having breakfast together to soak up the last moments before you're officially married. It can start with you and your bridal party sharing mimosas before you get the day rolling, or it can start as soon as your hair and makeup team gets started.

Getting ready is an important time. This is when you start to feel the excitement happening. Capturing the getting ready process is special

4

as it captures genuine moments spent with your family and friends. The moments spent getting ready with your loved ones are filled with laughter, shared stories, and heartfelt emotions. These are the precious memories that you'll want your photo and video team to capture and preserve for you. Whether it's the tender embrace of a parent, the supportive words of a friend, or the happy tears shared with your bridal party, each moment makes your wedding day uniquely yours. It's likely you'll forget these memories so having your photo and video team present during these moments will be such a gift in the future. Make sure to cherish this time just as much as the rest of your day!

Coverage Recommendation:

It's completely up to you whether or not you want your photo and video team present during the "getting ready" portion of the day. As a wedding photographer and videographer myself, we typically recommend at least one hour of coverage devoted to getting ready with a maximum of three hours depending on the events taking place that morning.

With that being said, here are the topics we will go over in this section:

- **Getting Ready Location**
- **Hair & Makeup Schedule for Brides and Bridesmaids**
- **Groomsmen Getting Ready**
- **Photo & Video Arrival Time**
- **Taking Time to Include Family**
- **The Details**
- **Gifts, Letters, Interviews**
- **Putting On Wedding Attire**
- **First Look**
- **Pre-Ceremony Bridal Party & Family Photos**
- **Transportation Between Locations**

Getting Ready Location

The getting ready location is very important. The farther away you are from the venue, the more time will be taken up on your timeline. The farther away you are from each other while getting ready, the more time will be added to your timeline. Try to get ready as close to each other as possible and as close to the venue as possible. You don't want your photo and video team to waste time traveling from one spot to the other.

You'll want to choose a place that has nice natural light coming in, has a decent amount of space so everyone can comfortably get ready, and so you can comfortably get into your wedding attire. You also want to make sure it's a clean area so that your footage and photos don't look messy. Or keep it real! Totally up to you!

If your venue doesn't have a bridal suite for you to get ready in, or if you're not happy with it, a cute airbnb is always a great option! Airbnb's are usually pretty neat and tidy and still give you that "homey" feeling. If you don't want or can't find an airbnb, a hotel room is also a great option. We encourage our couples to choose a location where you and your partner can get ready at the same location. Either in two different rooms at the same hotel, if you don't plan on getting ready together, or a front house and a back house. This will help your photo and video team save on travel time, ensure everyone stays on schedule, and they can easily and quickly jump back and forth from groomsmen to bridesmaids to capture everyone hanging out and enjoying their time together.

If you or a family member lives locally and the home meets these recommendations, this can add sentimental footage to your video and a sweet keepsake in your photos.

Hair & Makeup Schedule for Brides & Bridesmaids

Hair and makeup is one of the most important pieces to planning your wedding day timeline. If hair and makeup runs late, usually because a bridesmaid is running late, everything else on the timeline tends to run late. As soon as you meet with your hair and makeup team, be sure to ask them how much time they will need to complete your hair and makeup, along with anyone else who is planning to have hair and makeup done. Take a headcount of who will want their hair and makeup done early on in the planning stages. Ask everyone in your bridal party, including parents, siblings, in-laws, and anyone else who will be present while you are getting ready. Make sure not to leave anyone out so you can get an accurate time frame from your team.

To ensure you don't run late, you'll want to make sure your team is finished with your hair and makeup at least one hour before you need to put on your wedding attire. This will depend on the amount of events you have scheduled before it is time to put on your dress. If you have parents, siblings, friends helping you get ready, or bridal party getting ready with you, make sure they are all fully ready at least 30 minutes *before* you. You don't wanna have to wait on anyone. You should be the *very last one* finished with hair and makeup. *Disclaimer:* speak to your hair and makeup team about this to gather their opinion and make sure you're all on the same page. They are the experts so it's important to get their feedback when planning hair and makeup into the timeline.

Groomsmen Getting Ready

Since the groom and groomsmen don't usually have a team doing their hair and makeup, it could be fun to plan some "hanging out" photos. Here are some ideas:

- Playing poker
- Playing a video game
- Having a drink
- Telling stories
- Playing pool
- Hanging out by the pool
- Help each other get ties on
- Share marital advice

If you're on a tight schedule, simply getting washed up real quick and putting their ties and jackets on will do just fine for coverage! Make sure all button up shirts have been washed so you don't get the folded crease lines from the packaging. You don't want them opened up the morning of and then see the fold lines in your photos and video. Their shirts should also be ironed BEFORE the wedding day. Make sure everyone knows how to tie a tie/bow tie and/or a pocket square *before* the wedding day. Yes, people do take up time on the wedding day to YouTube "how to tie a tie". This will cause delays if even one person is not prepared.

Coverage Recommendation:
Groom and groomsmen getting ready photos are usually much easier and quicker than bride and bridesmaid getting ready photos. Depending on how many groomsmen you have and if you have any activities planned, it could

take approximately 30 minutes to 1 hour to photograph and film groomsmen getting ready.

Photo & Video Arrival Time

Decide on when you want your photo and video team to arrive for the day. Many women don't wanna be photographed or filmed without their "face on". If this is you, it's common for your coverage to start when you have about 30 minutes left with hair and makeup so that when you're photographed and filmed you're *mostly* ready and they can capture finishing touches. Because of this, we typically like to start the timeline as follows:

1. Arrive
2. Start with Detail shots of dress, accessories, invitations, rings, vow books, etc.
3. Then Groom and Groomsmen getting ready photos
4. And then Bride and Bridesmaid getting ready photos.

This gives the ladies a bit more time to get ready and the guys can get their photos out of the way and then relax until they're needed again.

Taking Time to Include Family

If you are close to your family and it won't be a burden on you, take time to include them. There won't be much time after the getting ready portion. The day goes by too fast. For mothers and daughters, this is the ONLY time you have one on one time throughout the ENTIRE day. This is the same for fathers and sons, and any parent and/or grandparents.

Here are some ideas of how you can include your family:

- Get/eat breakfast together
- Ask them to get their hair and makeup done with you
- Ask them to take a moment to share some words of advice with you
- Ask them to help you get into your wedding attire
- Ask them to take some behind the scenes photos and video for you on her phone
- Take selfies with them

You can include grandparents, parents, siblings, and anyone else special to you that won't be with you during "getting ready", to do a first look reveal with you in your wedding attire. If you do this, you'll wanna make sure they're all fully dressed in their wedding outfits.

I'll say it again, only include family if they are close to you and it won't be a burden on you. You do not want any stress or negativity on your wedding day so if including family and friends will add bad vibes to your mood then just don't do it!

Coverage Recommendation:
If you do have family and friends spending time with you and/or your fiance that morning, ask yourself, how important is it to get documentation

of them? If it is very important, make sure to notify your photo and video team so it can be included on the timeline. You don't want any moment to be forgotten. Coverage time will vary.

The Details

Details are items and accessories you want photographed on their own, typically as a flat lay photo. If there are any specific items you would like photographed, be sure to have it all ready in a box or a bag the day before so when your photo and video team arrive you can make sure nothing is lost or forgotten and you don't take up time trying to find things. You can even assign a bridesmaid, groomsmen, or family member to be in charge of the details bag/box so there's less for you to stress about.

Here is a list of ideas for "Details":

- Wedding Attire
- Rings
- Perfume/cologne
- Heirlooms
- Vow books
- Invitation suites
- Jewelry
- Watch
- Tie
- Shoes
- Cuff links

- A customized hanger or even a simple wooden hanger to hang wedding attire on
- Tie clip
- Socks
- Gifts
- Anything customized
- Florals

This is just a list of examples. You don't NEED to have any of these things photographed if you don't want to or if you don't have them.

Coverage Recommendation:

Depending on how many items you have, it could take approximately 30-45 minutes to photograph <u>and</u> film your details.

Gifts, Letters, Interviews

Before putting on your wedding attire, this is the perfect time to exchange any gifts and letters from one another and do video interviews. For the bride, you can wear a nice robe or your getting ready outfit. For the groom, he can wear his wedding attire with or without the jacket since he doesn't normally have a "getting ready" outfit like the bride does.

Gifts and letters for each other should be ready the night before or the morning of and kept with your box or bag of "details". You want to make sure you've exchanged these items BEFORE your photo and video team arrive so they don't use any extra time trying to get them at the last minute.

This is something you can have a parent or bridesmaid and grooms-men take care of for you so you're not tempted to open it too early.

For letters, it's a good idea to keep this private so you can cherish the moment and not be distracted by people or noise around you. You can choose to read it out loud and your video team can record you so they can capture and add the audio to your video or you can read it to yourself. This is when the tears come! If you do choose to use the audio for your video, it's important to ask your photographer to either silence their camera (turning the shutter sound off) so it doesn't make additional noise. The clicking sound, every time they take a photo, can be heard in your recording and it can be distracting to you as you're reading. If they cannot turn off the sound, you can decide if you're okay with that or if you would like to ask them not to take photos while you're reading since you'll have video coverage of that moment anyway. It's completely up to you!

Interviews are something you would do with your video team either in private or while you're hanging out with your wedding party during getting ready. This is a super special keepsake that can be added to your video so you can keep that story forever!

Typical interview questions could be:

- How did you two meet?
- How did you know you were in love?
- How did you know you wanted to marry this person?
- What is your proposal story?
- What do you love about this person?

Coverage Recommendation:
Approximately 15 minutes (each, bride & groom) for opening gifts and reading letters.

Approximately 5-10 minutes (each, bride & groom) for interviews.

Putting On Wedding Attire

If you and your fiance plan on having certain family or friends or wedding party members help you get your wedding attire on, be sure to notify them ahead of time so they can be fully dressed at least 30 minutes before you are ready to put your attire on.

For the bride, you can ask your mom to help you get your dress on, sister to help you put your jewelry on, and your made of honor to help you put your shoes on. Or you could have your mom do it all or your sister(s) do it all. Choose someone who's important to you so you could spend just a little more time with them. You can even have your grandma help with your jewelry! Or your mother-in-law, *if you like her*.

For the groom, he can have dad, brothers, sister, groomsmen, grandpa, grandma, whoever is important to him, to help him get his jacket on, his tie, and put his watch on for him. We usually like to save the boutonniere special for his mom to put on but she can be included at any point!

Coverage Recommendation:
Approximately 30-45 minutes for the bride getting dressed and about 20-30 minutes for the groom getting dressed.

If you wanna have a first look reveal in your wedding dress with your dad, add an additional 15 minutes after you're fully dressed. If the groom would like to do a first look with his mom, add another 15 minutes. If you're not close with your parents, choose someone you are close with, a best friend, a grandparent, a sibling, another relative, etc.

Or you can choose to forgo this option all together. If you would like to do a first look with your bridesmaids, add another 10 minutes.

Side note: if you have matching robes, slippers, pj's, or outfits for you and your bridesmaids, plan about 15 minutes into the timeline to take photos with your girls *before* you put on your wedding dress. You can also include mom, sisters, and your mother-in-law at this time for some extra photos. Make sure all robes or pj's have been washed so you don't get the folded crease lines from the packaging. You don't wanna open them all up, the morning of, and see the fold lines in your photos and video. Not cute! But also, not the end of the world.

First Look

A First Look is when the couple gets all dressed in their wedding attire and chooses to do a reveal of one another before the ceremony. Couple's like to do this so they can enjoy this moment in private before everyone arrives and have more time for "couple's portraits" before the ceremony. It's also a great way to ease the nerves.

If you don't feel comfortable reading your vows during the ceremony, a first look is also a great time for you to read vows to each other in private.

If you choose to forego a first look:

If you've always dreamed of seeing each other for the first time at the aisle, do it! It's your day and your decision!

Some things to keep in mind:

- You will have to take all group photos of the full bridal party, full family, and all the couple's portraits after the ceremony. If you do this, consider an earlier ceremony time so you have enough daylight for photos and video.
- You will need to have a longer cocktail hour in order to fit all the group photos. Consider having some games, Polaroids, or activities that will keep your guests occupied
- If reading vows during your ceremony was a concern but you don't wanna do a first look, you can always read vows in private after the ceremony.

Coverage Recommendation:
Approximately 45-60 minutes.

Pre-Ceremony Bridal Party & Family Photos

If there's time, try and get as many bridal party and family photos as possible before the ceremony. If you only have time for one, choose to do separate bridal party photos before the ceremony and then all the family photos after the ceremony.

You can get separate bridal party photos before the ceremony and then full bridal party photos after the ceremony. So you'd take all the bride and bridesmaid group photos and then singles of the bride with each bridesmaid. Then also take the groom and groomsmen photos and then singles of the groom with each groomsmen.

Example for Bride and Bridesmaids:
Photos 1-5: Group photos with Jane (bride) and Becky, Sarah, Bianca,

and Vanessa (bridesmaids)
    Photo 6: Jane & Becky
    Photo 7: Jane & Sarah
    Photo 8: Jane & Bianca
    Photo 9: Jane & Vanessa

<u>Example for Groom and Groomsmen:</u>

    Photos 1-5: Group photos with Michael (groom) and Bobby, Ian, Joe, and Josh (groomsmen)
    Photo 6: Michael & Bobby
    Photo 7: Michael & Ian
    Photo 8: Michael & Joe
    Photo 9: Michael & Josh

Coverage Recommendation:

Approximately 45 minutes of coverage is recommended for pre-ceremony bridal party photos if they are taken all together after a first look, or 30 minutes for each side if there's no first look, depending on the size of your bridal party.

If you choose to forgo a first look, and you have time, each of you can take your immediate family photos separately so that after the ceremony all you have to do is take one group photo of each side of the family, that includes the both of you, instead of all the different sets of family photos.

<u>Separate family photos example:</u>

Pre-Ceremony family photos with the bride would include: *(approx. 15 min)*

- Photo 1: Bride, mom, dad, sister, brother
- Photo 2: Bride, mom, dad
- Photo 3: Bride, mom
- Photo 4: Bride, dad
- Photo 5: Bride, siblings
- Photo 6: Bride, grandma, grandpa *(optional)*

Pre-Ceremony family photos with the groom would include: *(approx. 15 min)*

- Photo 1: Groom, mom, dad, sister, brother
- Photo 2: Groom, mom, dad
- Photo 3: Groom, mom
- Photo 4: Groom, dad
- Photo 5: Groom, siblings
- Photo 6: Groom, grandma, grandpa *(optional)*

If you choose to *have* a first look, your pre-ceremony family photos would look like this:

Groom's Side

- Photo 1: Groom, Bride, mom, dad, siblings
- Photo 2: Groom, Bride, mom, dad
- Photo 3: Groom, mom, dad
- Photo 4: Groom, mom
- Photo 5: Groom, dad
- Photo 6: Groom, siblings
- Photo 7: Groom, Bride, siblings
- *Optional, add in grandparents*

Bride's Side

- Photo 8: Groom, Bride, mom, dad, siblings
- Photo 9: Groom, Bride, mom, dad
- Photo 10: Bride, mom, dad
- Photo 11: Bride, mom
- Photo 12: Bride, dad
- Photo 13: Bride, siblings
- Photo 14: Groom, Bride, sibling
- *Optional, add in grandparents*

Coverage Recommendation:
Approximately 30 minutes total for both sides of the family.

Transportation Between Locations

Prepare ahead of time for any transportation between locations. Make sure transportation for you, your wedding party, and any other family that will be with you getting ready, is taken care of. Do a head count and assign drivers.

If you plan on going to a different location for formal portraits, be sure to know if your wedding party will be joining you or if it will just be the two of you. If it will just be the two of you, decide if you will be driving yourselves, if a bridal party member will be driving you, or if you will be hopping in the car with your photo and video team. Make sure ALL transportation is figured out BEFORE your wedding day so you don't have to take any extra time trying to make last minute arrangements since every minute counts!

Have all the addresses written down and search google maps to know the distance and how long it will take to go from one location to the next. If google maps says it will take 10 minutes to get to your venue from your getting ready location, add an additional 10 minutes of buffer time to count for possible traffic, construction, or any other delays. I recommend adding 15-20 minutes of buffer time for travel times longer than 30 minutes.

4

Ceremony

Things we will cover

- **Unplugged Ceremony**
- **Ceremony Start Time**
- **During the Ceremony**
- **First Kiss**

Unplugged Ceremony

An unplugged ceremony is one where the couple asks the guests to silence their phones and put them away during the entirety of the ceremony so they don't try to take their own photos or videos. When guests stick their arms out too far they can end up blocking you coming up or down the aisle and then your "down the aisle first look" dream shot is ruined. Or instead of seeing hands clapping and cheering during your first kiss you see a bunch of cell phones which doesn't make for great wall art.

You can personally announce this to your guests ahead of time, include the message in your invitations, and also ask your officiant to make an announcement to your guests before the ceremony gets started. You don't want the most important part of your day ruined by a guest's cell phone!

Ceremony Start Time

What time should you start your ceremony? First, check what time the sun is gonna set on your wedding day. You'll probably start with the sunset time <u>first</u> when planning out your timeline. For example, you can google "sunset time on November 11 in Arizona". If the sun is gonna set at 5:28pm that day, a good rule of thumb is to start your ceremony at least 3 hours before sunset. This would put your ceremony start time at 2:30pm. Your start time will depend on the following:

- How long do you expect your ceremony to last?
- How much family will you have taking photos after your ceremony?
- How big is your bridal party for photos after the ceremony?
- How important is it for you to join your guests in cocktail hour versus taking a longer time to do couple's portraits?
- What time is dinner expected to be ready?

Speak with your photo and video team and get their input on how long they believe it should take after you give them the answer to all these questions.

<u>Here's a sample:</u>

2:30 Ceremony Starts (*30 minute ceremony*)

3:00 Ceremony Ends

3:15 - 3:45 Family Photos (*assuming you started photos before the ceremony*)

3:45 - 4:15 Bridal Party Photos (*assuming you started photos before the ceremony*)

4:15 - 5:30 Couple's Portraits (*assuming you don't feel the need to be at cocktail hour*)

5:28 Sunset

6:00 Dinner

Speak with your whole team to plan this out. Speak with your officiant about how long your ceremony should take, decide if you want to join cocktail hour, and ask catering what time dinner should be ready and if it's flexible, and speak with your photo and video team to know about how long they feel they'll need for all the portraits. ***Once you know what time the sun is gonna set and you have the answer to the above questions, you're basically gonna work your way backwards from there to plan out your whole timeline.***

During the Ceremony

The most important event of your wedding day is the ceremony! This is when you actually get married. It's important not to rush this. I'm sure you're gonna want it to be over so that all you have to worry about is the dance party, but this is where you commit your lives to one another. You don't want it too short and definitely not too long. A good length is between 20-30 minutes.

Some couples like to do a sand ceremony, or a "tie the knot", or take communion if it's a religious ceremony. If these things are not something you're interested in but still want to make it more memorable, choose one or two people from both sides of your family to do a reading. This could be a poem or it could be marital advice. Make it your own!

Something else to think about is the officiant. This could be your Pastor, Bishop, etc. Another option is to have a close family member, parent, grandparent, or close friend officiate for you. We especially love this because it makes your ceremony even more sentimental! You'll want it to be someone who means a lot to you and maybe who had a great impact on your relationship. Do not choose a friend or family member simply because it's free, although that is a plus! Choose them because you trust them to make your ceremony special.

Lastly, your vows. We HIGHLY recommend you both write your own vows. I know this can sound intimidating or scary but TRUST ME! Your ceremony will be so much more special and your wedding video will be so much more beautiful if you do this! Be sure to give yourself enough time to write them. Try and have them written on your phone or in a notebook about a week before your wedding. Then on your wedding day, if you'd like, you can have your photo and video team document you writing your vows in your vow book. At times, couples end up not reading vows because they simply lost track of time. If you choose not to write your own vows, work with your officiant to make custom vows that you both read. That way, it's a little less scary but the vows are still special. GET VULNERABLE!

If you choose to write your vows in your vow books the morning of your wedding, add in 10 minutes each of coverage time during getting ready for this, depending on how long your vows are and how fast/slow you write.

First Kiss

Now you only get one shot at this so make that sucker count! Ask your officiant ahead of time to move off to the side when you do your first kiss so they're not oddly standing right behind you for your photos and video. Then make sure you HOLD it for a few seconds so your photo and video team doesn't miss it!

Once you've been announced, walk slowly down the aisle so you can look at your guests and really take in who's all there. This also gives your photo and video team a little more time to capture your excitement coming down.

If your venue allows, you can have guests throwing confetti or flower petals which makes for an even more beautiful exit! Then stop about midway down the aisle or at the very end of the aisle to give another kiss so your team can see your guests cheering behind you while they take photos and video. Remember again to hold it. At least count to three.

5

Post Ceremony

T hings we will cover:

- **Signing the Marriage License**
- **Family Portraits**
- **Wedding Party Portraits**
- **Couple's Portraits**

Signing of the Marriage License

Most couples sign their marriage license immediately after their ceremony. They'll sign it, have their witnesses sign it, pose with the license, drink some water, eat some snacks, and then get ready for family photos.

Coverage Recommendation:

Approximately 20 minutes of coverage recommended for this.

Be sure to notify your witnesses ahead of time and make sure they follow you immediately after the ceremony. Do not let them leave ANYWHERE.

While you're signing your license, you can have your whole wedding party with you, parents with you, or it could be just the two of you and your witnesses.

Then, ask your DJ ahead of time to make an announcement for notified family members and the bridal party to stay at the ceremony location for family photos and bridal party photos. Make sure to personally notify all these people ahead of time so no one starts wondering off and anyone who has not been asked ahead of time to stay, can leave to attend cocktail hour. You do NOT wanna have to wait for aunt Sue to come back from her car because she got cold and needed her jacket. We're always waiting for at least two people to come back from the bathroom. Tell everyone to make sure they have everything they need, use the bathroom before the ceremony, and stay put while they wait for you to come back.

Family Portraits

Coverage Recommendation:
Approximately 30 minutes, minimum, of coverage recommended. A good rule of thumb is to count 1 minute per head. If you have 20 people total taking family photos, then you should plan for 20 minutes, or round up to 30 minutes to be safe.

It's very important to put together a family shot list for your photographer. A family shot list is a list of all the names of your family and friends that you want to be photographed with during family portraits. Then, you'll list out the combinations of photos that you want taken.

Here's an example of what our form looks like:

"Please list the immediate side of the family, by name and relationship, of people getting photographed. If there are step families, be sure to group who will be getting photographed together."

Rebecca (spouse 1) Sample List:

Set 1

- Gabriela (mom) Bobby (stepdad)
- Bionca (sister) Anthony (brother in law), Ariel (niece)
- Michael (brother) Monique (sister in law), Jayden (nephew), Jaycob (nephew)
- Nicole (step sister) Ron (brother in law) Aubrey (niece) Autumn (niece)
- Isabella (sister)
- Robert (brother)
- Oscar (grandpa) Lucy (grandma)

Set 2

- Robert (Dad) Diane (step mom)
- Bionca (sister) Anthony (brother in law), Ariel (niece)
- Michael (brother) Monique (sister in law), Jayden (nephew), Jaycob (nephew)
- Marissa (sister)
- Joshua (brother)

21 People total for Rebecca's side

Cameron (Spouse 2) Sample List
<u>Set 3</u>

- Gwen (mom) Paul (dad)
- Cassidy (sister) Matt (brother in law) Mila (niece) Indy (niece)
- Cassandra (sister) Jess (brother in law) Mason (nephew) Jaxon (Nephew)
- Caitlyn (sister)

11 people total for Cameron's side

This is what the list of names look like, and here's an example of what your photographer would put together *with* you:

Rebecca's family portraits (set 1)

Photo 1: Cameron, Rebecca, Gabriela (mom), Bobby (stepdad), Bionca (sister), Anthony (brother in law), Ariel (niece), Michael (brother), Monique (sister in law), Jayden (nephew), Jaycob (nephew) Nicole (step sister), Ron (brother in law), Aubrey (niece), Autumn (niece), Isabella (sister), Robert (brother)

Photo 2: Cameron, Rebecca, Gabriela (mom), Bobby (stepdad), Bionca (sister), Michael (brother), Nicole (step sister), Isabella (sister), Robert (brother)

Photo 3: Cameron, Rebecca, Gabriela (mom), Bobby (stepdad)

Photo 4: Rebecca, Gabriela (mom)

Photo 5: Rebecca, Bobby (stepdad)

Photo 6: Rebecca, Bionca (sister), Michael (brother), Nicole (step sister), Isabella (sister), Robert (brother)

Photo 7: Rebecca, Bionca (sister), Nicole (step sister), Isabella (sister)

Photo 8: Rebecca, Bionca (sister)

Photo 9: Rebecca, Nicole (step sister)

Photo 10: Rebecca, Isabella (sister)

Photo 11: Rebecca, Michael (brother), Robert (brother)

Photo 12: Rebecca, Michael (brother)

Photo 13: Rebecca, Robert (brother)

You get the idea? You would do this for set 2 and set 3 and any other sets of family and friends you'd like to be photographed with. You don't *have* to do all those different groupings but parents usually like to have them and many people like to use those photos for birthday posts when sharing to social media and for gifting to family.

Having this list sent to your photographer, or printed out, will make things so much easier, smoother, and quicker. Your photographer will then be able to shout out all the names of who's expected in the first photo, and then let the next group of people know who will be up next. Not having a list means you have to wing it on the day of. It's super unorganized, you're going back and forth with people, you might forget a group combination you wanted, it's more time consuming, and much more stressful.

Keep in mind, the above example is just for ONE set. You can see how tedious this can get. This doesn't even include aunts, uncles, cousins, or close friends. This is why we highly recommend you try and get as many of these photos as you possibly can before the ceremony. It's also a good idea to run this by parents and/or other important family members to see if THEY have a photo combination they would like that hasn't been thought of. You don't want any unhappy family members. BUT, this is *your* day, so if you don't wanna spend forever taking a bunch of family photos just because mom wants her cousin to take a photo with you who you haven't seen in years, then don't do it! It's very common for couples to take photos with immediate family only, and then take photos with everyone else during the reception so you have plenty of time for bridal party photos and couple's portraits.

So, ask yourself these questions when planning out family portraits:

- How long do I wanna spend taking family portraits?
- Can I do any of these before the ceremony?
- Can I save some group combinations for during the reception?
- Do I want a group photo of both sides of our immediate family?

Since there are 32 people total listed above, you'd plan for 32 minutes of coverage in your timeline for family portraits, or round up to 35 minutes. This is assuming of course that all the family was where they were supposed to be and you didn't need to wait on anyone. Speak with your photographer about all of this. They will be the best one to let you know how quickly they can get through family photos for you.

This is something your photographer should be helping you with. A shot list will help stay on track with the timeline and make sure you can run through all the family portraits as quickly as possible. Your shot list should include names and sets of photos that you want captured to ensure no one is forgotten. Your photographer will usually ask you to put this together for them.

As I mentioned above, notify specific family members ahead of time that they'll be in the family photos. They need to stay put so no one wanders off and you're not waiting on anyone getting a drink or going to the bathroom. The longer it takes to get family photos done, the less time you will have for couple's portraits.

You can announce to your guests yourself, or you can also ask your photographer ahead of time to announce to your family and guests that there will be no cell phone photos allowed to be taken during family photos. Family members standing on the sides will want to jump in and say "hold on, let me take a cell phone photo of you guys" or "hold on, can you take a photo of us with my phone?". If you're pressed for time, 100% do not allow this to happen. This takes up too much time for your photographer to stop and take a cell phone photo or to stop and allow someone else to jump in and get their photo. Cell phone photos can be taken during the reception. However, this is your day! So if you wanna allow guests to stop your photographer and take their own photos, let your photographer know, and then add an additional 15 minutes for this.

Wedding Party Portraits

Coverage Recommendation:
Approximately 30-60 minutes of coverage recommended

As a reminder, to save time after the ceremony, it's a good idea to get bridesmaid and groomsmen portraits (individuals and group) separately before the ceremony to ensure you have enough time for couple's portraits after the ceremony. This usually takes about 30 minutes for each (pre-ceremony). Then you would take the big group portraits after the ceremony since the light is usually much better (another 30 minutes, post-ceremony) with a variety of poses.

If you do not take any bridal party portraits before the ceremony, depending on the size of your bridal party, plan for about 45-60 minutes of coverage time after family portraits. Remember, you don't *need* to take all these photos if you don't want to. This is your day! You plan it however you want it!

Couple's Portraits

Couple's portraits are one of the most important parts of your day! They may even be the only photos from your wedding day that you actually print out and hang on your wall. Remember, if you choose to have a first look, your photo and video team should capture some couple's portraits at that time as well as after the ceremony. If you choose not to have a first look, you'll definitely wanna make sure there's enough time planned for after the ceremony. 60 minutes is a good enough time to get a decent variety of poses. Let your photo and video team know if you plan on moving around the venue or even leaving the venue for couple's portraits.

For some couples, joining their guests during cocktail hour is very important to them. If this is you, AND you choose to not have a first look, this means you would only have about 15-30 minutes for couple's portraits after the ceremony.

This is enough time to get a few good shots but not enough time to really document your attire, bridals, beautiful poses, landscape photos, etc.

One option would be to have bridals and/or couple's portraits on a separate day, either before or after the wedding day. This is a great option for couples who really want to prioritize couple's portraits and may not have enough time on the wedding day.

Questions to ask yourself:

1) How important are couple's portraits to me?
2) How much time do I wanna spend taking couple's portraits on my wedding day?
3) Is it important for me to join my guests during cocktail hour?
4) Would it be best for my overall wedding day experience to book a session before or after my wedding day?

These are very important questions that will make a big impact on your wedding day experience so speak with your fiance about this and decide together how you want to move forward. Then speak with your photo and video team for their input.

6

The Reception

Special Events

Your reception coverage will be determined by the amount of "Special Events" you have taking place during your reception. Special Events are events like father daughter dance, cake cutting, first dance, toasts, etc. Here is a full list of possible events. We won't go into each one of them but I listed approximate times next to the event:

- Grand Entrance (*5 mins*)
- First Dance (*5 mins*)
- Opening Remarks / Welcome / Prayer for dinner (*5 mins*)
- Toasts (*time will vary, should be no longer than 15 minutes*)
- Parent Dances (*6 mins*)
- Choreographed Dances (*5 mins*)
- Photo booth/games (*no real set time*)
- Bouquet Toss (*10 mins*)

- Garter Toss (*10 mins*)
- Anniversary Dance (*depends on # of songs played, shouldn't be more than 15 min*)
- Honeymoon Fund/Dollar Dance (*depends on # of songs played, no more than 30 min*)
- Group Photos with guests (*time will vary*)
- Desserts/Cake Cutting (*5 mins*)
- Final Dance (*5 mins*)
- Send-Off/Grand Exit (sparkler exit) (*30 mins*)

This is YOUR wedding and ultimately it's up to you how your reception should go! You can choose to do some of these, none of these, or all of them! If you have any ideas that are not listed here just be sure to notify your photo and video team so they are prepared to document.

If you wanna step away from traditions like the bouquet toss and the garter toss, one option would be to do an anniversary dance instead. This is where all the couples get out on the dance floor and dance to a romantic song and the DJ will ask couples to leave the dance floor if they've been married for 1 year, 5 years, 10 years, then 20 years, etc., until the couple being married the longest is the last one on the dance floor. That couple can then offer a quick word of advice on how to stay married.

Some couples don't like cake. Instead they choose desserts like churros, donuts, or even ice cream! Again! This is YOUR wedding day! You do what you want!

Dinner

Planning out dinner needs to be top of mind when putting your Reception timeline together. This is because most couples like to start toasts during dinner. Most dinner options include buffet style, plated dinner, or food truck. Buffet and plated dinner usually take about the same amount of time. The benefit of having a plated dinner vs a buffet style or food truck is that most guests will be in their seats the whole time and you can start toasts a bit earlier than you would if you had a buffet or food truck. This is because with a buffet and food truck, people are out of their seats. This usually means that you would start toasts when at least most people are back to their seats which can take longer.

Toasts/Speeches

Toasts are another thing that can push back a timeline and run behind. The more people you ask to speak, the longer it will take. Whoever you ask to give a toast, give them a time limit. Two minutes is the sweet spot. It's not too long or too short. Parents and grandparents don't usually like to be given a time limit so consider giving them no more than five minutes.

Coverage Recommendation:
It should take no more than 10-15 minutes total for toasts.

Anything longer than that can make your guests antsy and can feel like the reception is dragging. The longer it takes for dancing to begin the less excitement there is. Be strict with your time limit. You don't wanna end up blaming specific people for the reason why your reception timeline is running late.

To achieve this, try not to ask too many people to give toasts. If you need to evenly space out speakers, you can ask one or two people to speak during your ceremony, during the "welcome/opening remarks", and then whoever is remaining can speak during your allotted time for toasts.

Speak with your DJ about when you should start toasts. Your DJ is usually the one to announce all the special events throughout your reception, including toasts. If you're on a tight timeline, or if you are already running behind, ask him to be strict about the toast's start time. You don't NEED absolutely everyone to be seated before you begin toasts. For the most part, your guests will take their seats when they hear that toasts are starting.

If you worry that your toast givers will have too much to drink by the time toasts are to begin, or if you would rather have an uninterrupted dinner, consider starting toasts before dinner starts. Speak with your photo and video team about this before you make a decision. They will need to let you know if they will be ready with all their equipment. Videographers need time to set up cameras, recorders, and possibly lights in order to record toasts. So speak to them first to make sure this would even be an option for you.

Open Dancing

Reception dancing is everyone's favorite part of the night! Depending on the type of crowd you have, dancing can either pick up pretty quickly, or it can take a good while before the floor gets filled, or it may not ever get fully filled. This is going to depend on two things, your guests and your DJ. If the majority of your guests are on the younger side, you may have more of a dancing crowd. If a majority of guests are on the older side it may take longer for the floor to fill up. OR if dancing is in your culture (*like Latinos*), the age won't even matter! They'll wanna be on the dance floor all night! What will matter then is your DJ. The NUMBER ONE thing that will kill your night is the DJ. Invest in a great DJ! Don't say you weren't warned! If you have a terrible or inexperienced DJ, no one will be dancing.

The reason I say all this is because, in regards to your timeline, you'll want your photo and video team to have at least one solid hour to document open dancing. The longer it takes people to get out onto the dance floor, the less time and the less footage your photo and video team have to work with. This is especially a bigger deal for your videographer since people enjoy watching themselves dance in their wedding video. If no one or not enough people are dancing, they may not have enough or any footage to include in your video.

Coverage Recommendation:

If you hired a great DJ and you have a dancing crowd, one hour of coverage for reception dancing should be enough. If you don't have much of a dancing crowd or you had to hire a lower level DJ, I'd plan for two hours of coverage to be safe. This is only if coverage of reception dancing is important to you.

If you don't plan on having a Grand Exit (more detail in the next section) then you may not need to have your photo and video team stay for the whole night, unless you absolutely want them to. If cake cutting is your last event on the timeline, make sure to plan in enough time for them to cover dancing, and then they can leave for the night.

Grand Exit

A Grand Exit is when the couple plans some sort of farewell to the guests. Usually the guests will line up in two lines while you and your spouse come down the aisle with your getaway car at the end of the aisle. Examples of this would be a sparkler exit, where your guests hold out sparklers above you as you come down the aisle. You can have them throw flower petals, hold long sticks with ribbon at the end, glow sticks, blow bubbles, or even toss balloons (non helium).

Coverage Recommendation:
It can take a while to get everyone lined up and supplies passed out, so plan no less than 30 minutes of coverage for this. This is where your timeline would end, along with coverage from your photo and video team.

7

Planning Out Your Timeline

Remember, no two weddings are the same. Every couple is different, every venue is different, and every photo and video team is different. Just because something is written in this guide doesn't mean it's a concrete fact.

We've provided some sample timelines for you to review that will help give you an idea of how a wedding day, with and without certain events, could flow. Timing and order of events will vary per couple and per photo and video team.

We typically plan out timelines starting with sunset and then plan around that.

Sunset time listed on the sample timelines are subject to change depending on the day you're getting married.

Sample Timelines

12 HOUR TIMELINE - with first look

This timeline is based on the wedding date of June 30, 2023. This couple was married at a wedding venue where the full bridal party had early access to their bridal suite to get ready. This is why you don't see any travel time listed in the timeline. Because of this, they were able to add in a few extra events before their ceremony started. You also see they had more daylight to work with since sunset was at 7:42pm. It was important to the couple to join their friends and family at cocktail hour so they had a first look and were able to knock out a good chunk of couple's portraits, bridal party portraits, and family portraits before the ceremony. Lastly, their venue allowed them to stay until 11:00pm which means they had more time for reception dancing.

10:00 Girls start hair and makeup
   11:00 Photo and Video team arrives
   11:15 Shoot detail shots
   11:30 Photos of guys hanging out
   12:00 Groom gets dressed
   12:15 Groom opens gift
   12:20 Groom reads letter
   12:30 Groomsmen Photos
   1:00 Bride done with hair and makeup
   1:10 Photos of girls hanging out
   1:20 Bride opens gift
   1:25 Bride reads letter
   1:30 Bride puts on Dress
   2:00 First look with Bridesmaids
   2:15 Head to first look location (on venue property)
   2:30 Bride & Groom First Look

2:40 Couple's Portraits
3:15 Bridal Party Photos

* Bridesmaid photos
* Groomsmen Photos
* (full bridal party photos after ceremony)

3:45 Immediate Family Photos
4:00 Couple Tucked Away

* Guests being seated

4:30 Ceremony Starts
5:00 Ceremony Ends
- Take a moment to yourselves
- Sign marriage license
5:15 Remaining Family & Friends Portraits
5:45 Full Bridal Party Portraits
6:00 Couple's Portraits
6:45 Bride & Groom joins guests at cocktail hour
7:15 Prep for grand entrance
7:20 Grand Entrance
7:25 First Dance
7:30 Opening Remarks
7:30 Dinner
7:42 Sunset
8:00 Toasts
8:20 Parent Dances
8:30 Open Dancing
9:00 Cake cutting
9:05 Bouquet toss

9:15 Garter toss
10:25 Final Song/Dance
10:30 Get ready for Sparkler Exit
11:00 Finished / Photo & Video team end

<u>Something to think about:</u> While it does look like they were able to get a lot of events in the timeline, this is considered a very "tight" timeline. Meaning, instead of being relaxed, this couple was just go, go, go, the whole day. Pros: they were able to do everything they wanted. Cons: since there were so many things planned, the day feels like it goes by faster and you're constantly on the go instead of being able to relax and take your time. If you're prone to anxiety, I wouldn't suggest you take this approach. Less is more.

12 HOUR TIMELINE - no first look

This timeline is based on the wedding date of April 1, 2023. This couple did not do a first look but still had time to do bridal party photos and some family photos before the ceremony. Because of this, they didn't need much time after the ceremony for more family and bridal party photos.

Reception dancing was very important to them so they made sure to have dinner start at 6:00pm since the venue's "no noise" policy started at 10:00pm. They wanted to have enough time for dancing. This did cut down time for couple's portraits but since they weren't spending lots of time with family and bridal party photos, they were still able to get 45 minutes of couple's portraits.

9:00 Girls start hair and makeup
   10:00 Photo & Video Coverage Time Begins at bride's airbnb

- Detail shots of Yesenia's dress, shoes, accessories, etc.
- Photos/Video of girls hanging out

10:45 Photo & Video team leave to venue

- 8 min. drive

11:00 Photo & Video team arrive to venue bridal suite

- Groom and groomsmen also arrive

11:30 Photos of guys hanging out in bridal suite

- Blake's detail shots

12:00 Blake start getting dressed

- Best Man helps Blake put on his tie
- Groomsmen get dressed

12:30 Groomsmen Photos

- Group photos & one on one photos with groomsmen
- Single photos of Blake

12:30 All girls done with hair and makeup

- Pack up cars

1:00 Girls leave airbnb to venue

    1:15 Photos of Blake with Parents and sister

    1:30 Girls arrive to bridal suite

- Photos of girl's touch ups
- Hanging out in bridal suite
- Matching pajamas photos

2:00 Yesenia put on wedding dress

- Help from mom, sisters, and mother-in-law

2:45 Bridesmaids Photos

- One on one photos
- Single photos of Yesenia

3:15 Photos of Yesenia with close family

- Reference "shot list"

3:30 All bridal party tucked away

- Guests seated at ceremony site

4:00 Ceremony starts

- Take communion

4:30 Ceremony over

- Sign marriage license
- Cocktail hour starts

4:40 Family Photos

- Immediate family only, reference "shot list"

4:50 Full Bridal Party Photos
    5:00 Couple's Portraits
    5:45 Finished with Couple's Portraits
    5:50 Grand Entrance
    5:55 First Dance

- Choreographed salsa dance

6:00 Dinner

- In-n-Out Food truck & Taco Man

6:30 Toasts

- Best Man
- Yesenia's Sister
- Maid of Honor
- Thank You from Blake & Yesenia

6:45 Parent Dances

- mother/son dance
- mother/daughter dance

6:50 Dollar Dance

- 2 songs

7:00 Open Dancing
  7:12 Sunset
  8:00 Bouquet Toss
  8:05 Cake Cutting
  9:55 Final Dance Song
  10:00 End of Reception/Photo and Video team end

- No grand exit

Something to think about: this timeline had less events in the day which helped the couple slow down and really take in the whole day which is exactly what they wanted. If this timeline is ideal for what you want, but you're concerned about getting enough couple's portraits, consider booking a next day session or a few days later or even a few days/week before your wedding day, to do wedding attire portraits. Couple's choose to do this when they don't wanna be spending the whole day taking photos. They would rather spend their day with their family and friends. This way, you get both!

8 HOUR TIMELINE - with first look

This timeline is based on the wedding date of March 11, 2023. Since this couple chose to have an 8 hour photo and video package, coverage started at 2:00pm at the venue. They didn't get any coverage of "getting ready".

They were really limited on light since they had a 5:00 pm ceremony start time and sunset started at 6:32pm. And since they wanted to do toasts *before* dinner they planned a first look and were able to do ALL family photos and bridal party photos before the ceremony. Because of this, they were able to focus the limited time they had after the ceremony to just shoot couple's portraits.

9:00 Girls getting ready

- Make sure dresses are steamed

11:00 Guys Getting Ready

- Make sure everyone knows how to tie a tie

1:00 All Girls Get Dressed
   1:20 ALL girls COMPLETELY dressed and ready to go

- Bridesmaids, mom, mother-in-law

1:30 Girls head down to parking lot

- Pack up car

1:40 Leave Hotel to Venue
   1:50 Arrive to Venue
   2:00 Photo & Video Team Start
   2:00 Bride, bridesmaids, & mothers in bridal suite
   2:15 Ivy puts on dress

- Mom and mother-in-law help

2:30 First look with Ivy & her dad
   2:45 Alonso & Groomsmen arrive at venue

- Fully dressed

3:15 Ivy & Alonso first look
   3:30 Pictures

- Family Photos (see "shot list")
- Bridal Party Photos

4:30 Ivy & Alonso tucked away

- Guests start arriving

5:00 Ceremony Starts
   5:30 Ceremony Over

- Sign marriage license
- Cocktail hour

5:45 Couple's Portraits
   6:20 Finished with Couple's Portraits

- Guests seated in reception area

6:30 Grand Entrance

- Bridal party (6 girls, 6 guys)

6:32 Sunset
6:35 Photo Rush Each Table
6:40 Toasts

- Ivy's mom & Dad
- Maid of honor
- Best man
- Alonso's mom & dad

7:00 Dinner

- Buffet (150 guests)

8:00 First Dance
8:05 Parent Dances

- Father/Daughter Dance
- Mother/Son Dance
- Not using whole song

8:10 Open Dancing
9:00 Cake Cutting
10:00 Photo & Video team end
10:15 Bar closing
10:30 Last Dance/Sparkler Exit
11:00 Ivy & Alonso Leave Venue

Their reception ended at 11:00pm but since they booked an 8 hour package, coverage ended at 10:00pm even though we would miss the sparkler exit, but the couple was okay with that.

8 HOUR TIMELINE - no First Look

This timeline is based on the wedding date of March 13, 2023. This is a pretty tight timeline. The couple didn't wanna do a first look and didn't have time before the ceremony to do any bridal party or family photos. Because of this, ALL family, bridal party photos, and couple's portraits were taken after the ceremony. They also wanted to join family and friends at cocktail hour. Since they had a 5:00 pm ceremony start time and sunset was at 6:36pm, they had very limited time for all their photos.

12:00 Sydnie & PJ arrive at venue separately
   12:00 Hair and Makeup Start (2 person team)

- Artist 1 Start with Sydnie's mom
- Artist 2 Start with Sydnie
- Bridesmaids (4) get started AFTER mom and Sydnie

2:30 Photo and Video Team Start

- Detail shots of Sydnie's dress, shoes, etc
- Flat lays

3:00 Detail shots of PJ getting dressed

- Hanging out with guys/family having drinks
- 4 groomsmen

3:15 PJ read letter from Sydnie
   3:00 Sydnie's mom done with hair and makeup

- Sydnie's mom get dressed

3:30 Sydnie done with hair and makeup
　3:45 ALL bridesmaids done with hair and makeup

- Photos of girls in matching robes and slippers
- Bridesmaids get dressed

4:00 Sydnie gets in dress

- Mom helps

4:20 Sydnie first look with dad
　4:25 Sydnie reads letter from PJ
　4:30 Detail shots of ceremony

- Sydnie and PJ tucked away in bridal suites

5:00 Ceremony Starts
　5:30 Ceremony Over

- Sign marriage license
- Cocktail hour

5:40 Family Photos

- See "shot list"

5:50 Bridal Party Photos
　6:00 Couple's Portraits
　6:30 Couple joins family and friends at cocktail hour
　6:36 Sunset
　6:55 Grand Entrance

7:00 Dinner
7:45 Toasts

- Sister of Groom
- Sister of Bride
- Best Man

8:00 First Dance

- Father/Daughter Dance
- Mother/Son Dance
- Cake Cutting

8:15 Open Dancing
9:30 Final Dance
9:35 Set up sparkler exit
9:45 Sparkler Exit
10:00 Photo & Video Team Finished

Something to think about: This timeline is for you if you'd rather not have a bunch of events planned, don't wanna spend all day in front of the camera, and would rather enjoy your day with family and friends. Your overall wedding day experience is more important than having a million photos taken.

Which Wedding Package Should I Choose?

It's gonna come down to two things:

1. Which events do I want documented?
2. What can I afford?

You *can* squeeze a bunch of events in a short timeline as long as you know that you *will* feel rushed on your wedding day. If an eight or even a six hour wedding day package is what you can afford, that's okay!

If you don't wanna feel rushed but can't afford a twelve hour package, then ask yourself, "what are the top three most important events/moments I don't wanna forget?" *(not including the ceremony)*. In other words, "What will I regret not having photos and video of?" Then plan your coverage time around those moments. It's better to skip less important moments than to be stressed out on your wedding day.

The day goes by so fast! If you can afford it, a 12 hour wedding day package is ideal if you wanna remember your full wedding day. Having 12 hours of coverage doesn't mean you'll be posing for twelve hours, it means you'll have your team there to document everything for you so you don't have to think twice about it. It's a gift you'll always be able to look back on.

Also know, not everyone needs 12 hours. What's important to one couple isn't important to another. You don't need to be sold on a larger package if you don't need it. This is why it's important to hire a photo and video team you trust that can walk you through this decision. *They* should be the experts here. They should be able to walk you through a whole day and help you decide which option is best for you.

8

Conclusion

Everything we've covered here should help you put together a rough timeline for your wedding day.

If you've already chosen the amount of hours in your wedding package with your photo and video team, but after reading this guide you feel you may need to adjust your package, just ask your team.

Working with an experienced planner is a huge help! Usually, they'll ask for your notes and input and then put a timeline together for you. If you don't have a planner, your photo and video team will sometimes assist with putting your timeline together.

If anything is causing you stress, then don't do it! You wanna remember your wedding day as the best day of your life! You don't wanna finish the night and say "we got through it" or "it's finally over".

REMEMBER, this is YOUR wedding day. Your timeline can be as jam packed or as open as you want it to be. It's okay if you want every minute planned and it's okay if you don't. Your photo and video team doesn't *have* to document you all day and it's okay if they do! This is the day you'll remember for the rest of your life, do what's only important to you! You do you!